16 95

D1305394

MONSTERS OF THE ANIMAL KINGDOM

VAMPIRE BATS

Rachel Lynette

PowerKiDS
press
New York

For Adam

Published in 2013 by The Rosen Publishing Group, Inc.
29 East 21st Street, New York, NY 10010

First Edition

Editor: Jennifer Way
Book Design: Greg Tucker

Photo Credits: Cover, pp. 4–5, 22 Michael Lynch/Shutterstock.com; p. 4 Katarzyna Citko/Shutterstock.com; p. 6 Carsten Peter/National Geographic/Getty Images; p. 7 Luiz Rocha/Shutterstock.com; p. 8 Tom McHugh/Photo Researchers/Getty Images; p. 9 (left) © www.iStockphoto.com/spxChrome; p. 9 (bottom), 20 Oxford Scientific/Getty Images; pp. 10, 11 (bat), 12–13 © Barry Mansell/Superstock; p. 11 (tree) nito/Shutterstock.com; pp. 14, 15 Bruce Dale/National Geographic/Getty Images; p. 16 Dr. Merlin Tuttle/Photo Researchers/Getty Images; p. 17 James H. Robinson/Photo Researchers/Getty Images; p. 18 salajean/Shutterstock.com; p. 19 Kobby Dagan/Shutterstock.com; p. 21 (left) Charles Masters/Shutterstock.com; p. 21 (bottom) Cynthia Kidwell/Shutterstock.com.

Library of Congress Cataloging-in-Publication Data

Lynette, Rachel.
 Vampire bats / by Rachel Lynette. — 1st ed.
   p. cm. — (Monsters of the animal kingdom)
 Includes index.
 ISBN 978-1-4488-9629-5 (library binding) — ISBN 978-1-4488-9716-2 (pbk.) —
 ISBN 978-1-4488-9725-4 (6-pack)
 1. Vampire bats—Juvenile literature. I. Title.
 QL737.C52L96 2013
 599.4'5—dc23
                              2012016371

Manufactured in the United States of America

CPSIA Compliance Information: Batch #W13PK5: For Further Information contact Rosen Publishing, New York, New York at 1-800-237-9932

CONTENTS

THIRSTY FOR BLOOD!

Can you imagine living on blood? If you were a vampire bat, that is exactly what you would do! Vampire bats are the only **mammals** that must drink blood to live.

There are more than 1,200 **species** of bats, but only three of them are vampire bats. The white-winged vampire bat and the hairy-legged vampire bat feed mostly on birds' blood. The common vampire bat is the most widespread species. Common vampire bats usually feast on larger mammals such as cows, pigs, and horses.

White-winged vampire bats and hairy-legged vampire bats feed on birds, including livestock like chickens.

A vampire bat's teeth are so small and so sharp that most of the time the animals the bat feeds on do not even wake up!

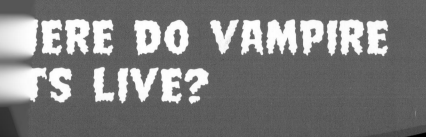

WHERE DO VAMPIRE BATS LIVE?

If you want to see vampire bats in the wild, you will need to go to Mexico, Central America, or South America. Vampire bats prefer the warm, humid forests and grasslands found in these places.

A colony of vampire bats on a tree trunk in Brazil.

One of the places vampire bats live are tropical forests, such as the Atlantic Forest in Brazil, shown here.

Vampire bats live together in groups, called colonies. There are 20 to 100 vampire bats in most colonies, but some colonies have 1,000 bats or more! Most vampire bat colonies make their homes in caves. A colony may also settle in a large, hollow tree, a mine shaft, an old well, or an empty building.

Most vampire bats are only about 3.5 inches (9 cm) long. With its wings spread out, a vampire bat is about 8 inches (20 cm) wide. Vampire bats have light, thin wings.

Unlike most other kinds of bats, vampire bats can easily crawl, jump, and even run along the ground.

This vampire bat is crawling on the ground. You can see its larger front limbs pulling its body along.

Left: The skin of a bat's wings is thin enough that you can see light shine through it. *Bottom*: Unlike other bats, vampire bats often fly close to the ground. They approach the animals they feed on from the ground.

Vampire bats crawl by using the strong forelimbs that are attached to their wings rather than their weaker back legs. These forelimbs have special clawed thumbs that help them crawl and climb.

SPECIAL SENSES

Like other bat species, vampire bats use **echolocation** to avoid flying into objects. The bats send out a high-pitched sound that echoes, or bounces, off objects in front of them. The echoes tell the bats how close they are to these objects.

The vampire bat's sense of echolocation is not as strong as that of other bats. Vampire bats use it to get around, not to find food.

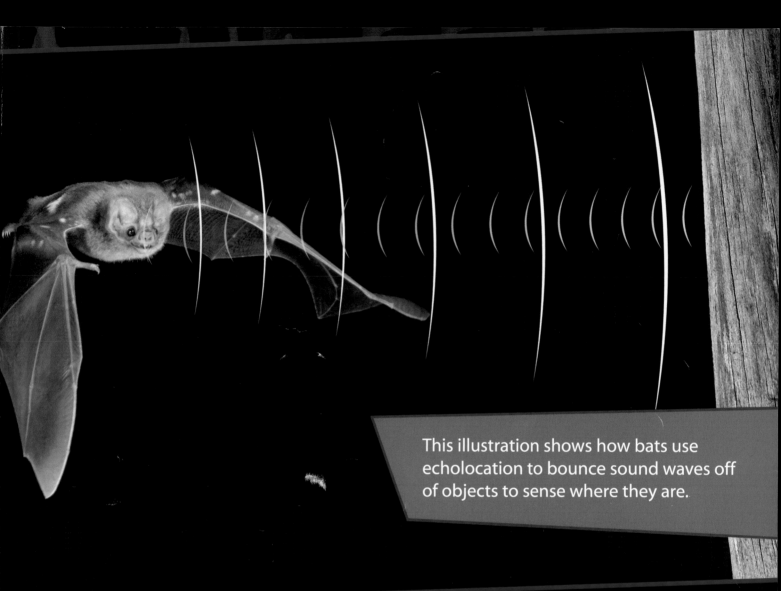

This illustration shows how bats use echolocation to bounce sound waves off of objects to sense where they are.

Vampire bats have a much stronger sense of smell than humans do. They can use their sense of smell to find **prey**. In a herd of animals, a vampire bat can use its sense of smell to find an animal it has preyed on before. A vampire bat often preys on the same animal again and again.

SCARY FACTS

1 The saliva of a vampire bat contains a substance that stops an animal's blood from **clotting**. The blood then keeps flowing so that the bat can drink it.

2 Vampire bat roosts are messy and smelly! The walls and floors are covered in slimy, digested-blood droppings.

3 Vampire bats often go to the bathroom while feeding. This makes it possible for them to drink more blood.

4 Vampire bats also go to the bathroom when they are finished feeding in order to lighten their blood-heavy bodies for flying.

5 Scientists are worried that as vampire bat populations grow, the bats may attack people more often. Attacks are on the rise in Peru.

6 A vampire bat must drink half its weight in blood every night.

7. Often, several vampire bats feast on the same animal at once.

8. In the 2005 movie *Vampire Bats*, **mutant** vampire bats attack the people of a small town.

9. A colony of 100 bats can drink the blood of 25 cows in a year!

A BLOODY DIET

Vampire bats live on blood. They cannot eat solid food because they have very narrow throats and zigzagging stomachs. A vampire bat needs about 2 tablespoons of blood each night.

Here you can see a vampire bat using its tongue to drink a cow's blood.

Vampire bats can sense heat with their noses. An animal's skin is warmer where the blood flows closest to the surface. This tells them the best place to bite.

A vampire bat feeds on just one animal each night. It uses its sharp **incisor** teeth to take a tiny bite. The bat drinks the animal's blood by using its tongue in the same way that a cat laps milk.

Vampire bats are **nocturnal**. This means they are active at night. During the day, vampire bats roost together, sleeping while hanging upside down. When they are not sleeping, they may spend time grooming each other's fur.

Adult vampire bats hunt for prey on their own and return to their roost after feeding.

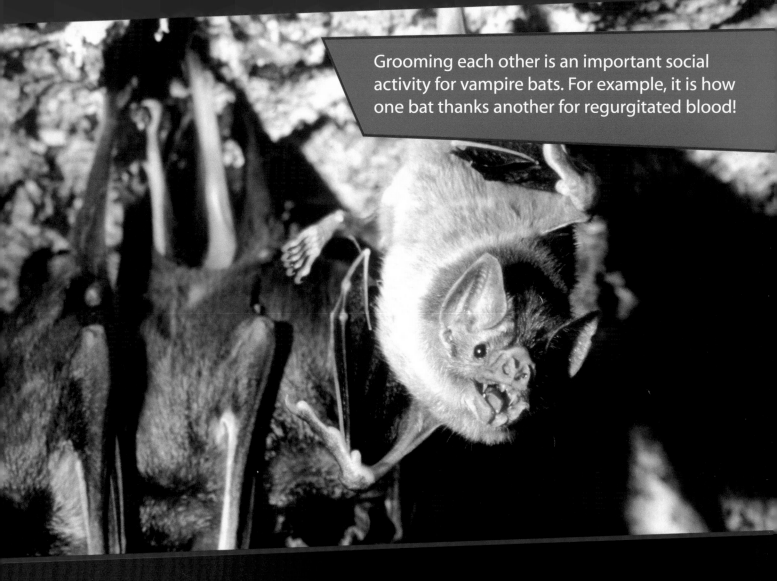

Grooming each other is an important social activity for vampire bats. For example, it is how one bat thanks another for regurgitated blood!

A bat cannot go more than about two days without feeding. Young bats that are still learning to hunt sometimes fail to get food. When this happens, other bats will help them by **regurgitating**, or vomiting, blood into the hungry bat's mouth. Drinking regurgitated blood sounds gross, but it saves many young bats from starving to death!

BABY BATS

After mating, a mother bat gives birth to one baby about seven months later. For the first two months, the baby drinks only its mother's milk. Then the mother starts to feed the baby regurgitated blood. At four months, the young bat starts to hunt with its mother.

Baby vampire bats are called pups. This person is holding a mother bat and her pup.

A mother vampire bat takes her young out to hunt prey that is resting for the night, such as these horses. At around five months, young bats will hunt on their own.

Mother vampire bats often help one another by feeding one another's babies. If a baby is orphaned, another mother may adopt it.

VAMPIRE BAT PREDATORS

A vampire bat risks its life every night when it goes out to hunt. Vampire bats have several **predators**, including eagles, hawks, owls, and snakes. Hawks have been seen waiting near the mouths of caves, ready to feast on returning vampire bats. Snakes may attack them from trees.

Vampire bats have to be careful when they are feeding. If this pig rolls over, it would crush this vampire bat!

Left: The barn owl is a vampire bat predator.
Bottom: The red-tailed hawk is found throughout North America and Central America. It preys on small animals including vampire bats.

Vampire bats also risk being squished to death by their sleeping prey. If the animal a vampire bat is preying on wakes up, it may roll over or step on the tiny bat. A vampire bat is so small that even the swat of a cow's tail could end its life.

FRIEND OR FOE?

Even though vampire bats do not take enough blood to kill an animal, they can still cause a lot of damage. The wounds they create while feeding can get **infected**. Vampire bats can also carry **rabies**. Rabies is a sickness that kills animals.

Many people are afraid of vampire bats. They may think of vampire bats as giant, blood-sucking monsters! There is little reason to worry about them, though, because vampire bats rarely bite humans.

As cattle ranches have spread across Mexico, Central America, and South America, vampire bat populations have spread along with them. Ranchers view the bats as pests.

clotting (KLAHT-ing) Thickening, of a liquid.

echolocation (eh-koh-loh-KAY-shun) A method of finding objects by producing a sound and judging the time it takes the echo to return and the direction from which it returns.

incisor (in-SY-zur) One of an animal's four front teeth used for cutting.

infected (in-FEK-ted) Became sick from germs.

mammals (MA-mulz) Warm-blooded animals that have backbones and hair, breathe air, and feed milk to their young.

mutant (MYOO-tunt) Having problems caused by changes in an animal's genes.

nocturnal (nok-TUR-nul) Active during the night.

predators (PREH-duh-terz) Animals that kill other animals for food.

prey (PRAY) An animal that is hunted by another animal for food.

rabies (RAY-beez) A deadly illness that wild animals can carry.

regurgitating (ree-GUR-juh-tayt-ing) Throwing food back up.

species (SPEE-sheez) One kind of living thing. All people are one species.

INDEX

WEBSITES

Due to the changing nature of Internet links, PowerKids Press has developed an online list of websites related to the subject of this book. This site is updated regularly. Please use this link to access the list:
www.powerkidslinks.com/mak/vbat/